WORLD BOOK

Uranus

AND

Neptune

THE ICE GIANTS

Contents

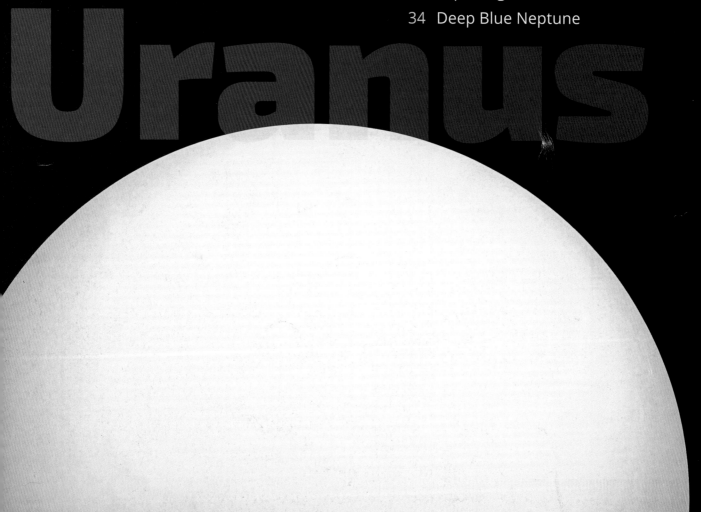

Neptune

If a word is printed in **bold letters that look like this** the first time it appears on any page, you will find the word's meaning in the Glossary beginning on page 60.

Astronomers use different kinds of photos to learn about such objects in space as planets. Many photos show an object's natural color. Other photos add false colors or show types of light that the human eye cannot normally see. When appropriate, the captions in this book will state whether a photo uses false color. Other photos and illustrations use color to highlight certain features of interest.

Uranus and Neptune

The Ice Giants

Far out in the most remote neighborhood of our **solar system** are the giant **planets** Uranus *(YUR uh nuhs)* and Neptune. These dark worlds were largely unknown to people in ancient times. Without a **telescope,** Uranus is barely visible in the night sky. It appears as a faint point of light. Neptune, the outermost planet in the solar system, cannot be seen at all without a telescope.

Uranus (left) and
Neptune (right)
are two giant, icy
worlds that lie in the
outermost reaches of
our solar system.

Uranus and Neptune have an
outer layer made mostly of
hydrogen and **helium** gas. But
astronomers have learned
that the interiors of Uranus and
Neptune are mainly heavier
substances. The planets are
made up mostly of a thick slushy
and icy **mantle** surrounding a
small, rocky **core.** For this reason,
astronomers call Uranus and
Neptune *ice giants.* Along with
Jupiter and Saturn, Uranus and
Neptune are the largest planets in
our solar system.

Lonely Giant
Uranus

Uranus is the

seventh planet from the sun.

It is one of the *outer planets* in the solar system. The other outer planets are Jupiter, Saturn, and Neptune.

Uranus as seen by NASA's Voyager 2 space probe

Uranus is

so far out

in the solar system that it takes 2 hours and 40 minutes for light from the sun to reach the planet!

A person zooming past Uranus in a spaceship would see a

smooth, blue-green

ball

surrounded by inky black space.

The orbit of Uranus

lies between the orbits of Saturn and Neptune. Saturn orbits closest to Uranus. But the two planets are not really close. In fact, the closest they get to each other is 10 times farther apart than Earth and the sun!

William and Caroline
Herschel

Discovery
of Uranus

Uranus was not known to people in ancient times. That is because Uranus is hard to see in the sky, even on the clearest nights.

The British astronomer William Herschel first observed Uranus with a telescope in 1781. At first, he thought he had discovered a new **comet** or **star.** He later realized that the object must be a planet. Herschel's discovery was not accepted until the German astronomer Johann Bode *(BOH duh)* confirmed that he had discovered a previously unknown planet.

Herschel wanted to name his new planet *Georgium Sidus* after Britain's King George III. But this name was not accepted by astronomers. Bode suggested a name based on the practice generally agreed upon of naming planets after gods or goddesses from ancient Greek and Roman mythology. Eventually, the name of an early sky god in Greek **mythology—** Uranus—came to be accepted.

FUN FACT

The radioactive element **uranium** was named after Uranus when it was discovered in 1789, just eight years after the planet was discovered.

URANUS

A Blue-Green
Planet

With the unaided eye, Uranus appears as a faint point of light in the night sky. When viewed through a telescope, Uranus appears as a small, pale, blue to blue-green disc.

The upper layers of Uranus are mostly hydrogen and helium, with a small amount of **methane** and traces of water and **ammonia.** The methane gives Uranus its pale blue color. Unlike Jupiter and Saturn, Uranus appears uniform in color. It does not have the stripes and swirls seen on Jupiter and Saturn.

Uranus appears entirely covered with clouds made up of tiny crystals of frozen methane. The crystals have formed out of the planet's **atmosphere.** Sunlight passes through the atmosphere and is reflected back out by the cloud tops. The methane clouds absorb the red light in sunlight and allow the blue light to pass through, giving the planet its color.

Uranus is shown against the Milky Way galaxy in this NASA image.

Size and Shape

Uranus is the third largest planet in the solar system. Only Jupiter and Saturn are larger.

The **diameter** of Uranus at its **equator** is 31,763 miles (51,118 kilometers), or a little less than **half the diameter of Saturn.**

1/2

Uranus is slightly larger in diameter than its neighbor Neptune. However, **Uranus has less mass** than Neptune. Mass is the amount of matter that an object has.

Compared with the sun, Uranus is very small. The diameter of the sun is about 864,000 miles (1.4 million kilometers). That means that **more than 25 planets the size of Uranus** could fit across the width of the sun.

Only Saturn is less **dense** than Uranus. Density is the amount of mass in a substance divided by its **volume** (the amount of space it takes). Uranus's density is about **1 $\frac{1}{4}$ times** that of water. The density of Uranus is only about $\frac{1}{4}$ that of Earth.

Uranus
and the Sun

Uranus's distance from the sun changes over time because its orbit is slightly *elliptical* (oval-shaped).

Uranus's average distance from the sun is about 1.8 billion miles (2.9 billion kilometers). That is more than 19 times as far from the sun as Earth!

Uranus is so far from the sun that it takes the planet a long time to complete its orbit. A **year** on Uranus—the time it takes to orbit the sun once—is 30,687 Earth **days,** or about 84 Earth years.

FUN FACT

Most of the other planets, including Earth, rotate on their axis in the same direction in which they orbit the sun. However, Uranus rotates in the

direction opposite

its orbit around the sun. Astronomers call this retrograde rotation. The planet Venus is the only other planet in our solar system with a retrograde rotation.

The length of a day on Uranus is about 17 ¼ Earth hours. It takes Uranus that long to *rotate* (spin around) one full turn on its **axis.** The axis is an imaginary line running through the center of a planet.

However, much of Uranus's atmosphere rotates even faster. An area near the south **pole** rotates once every 14 hours.

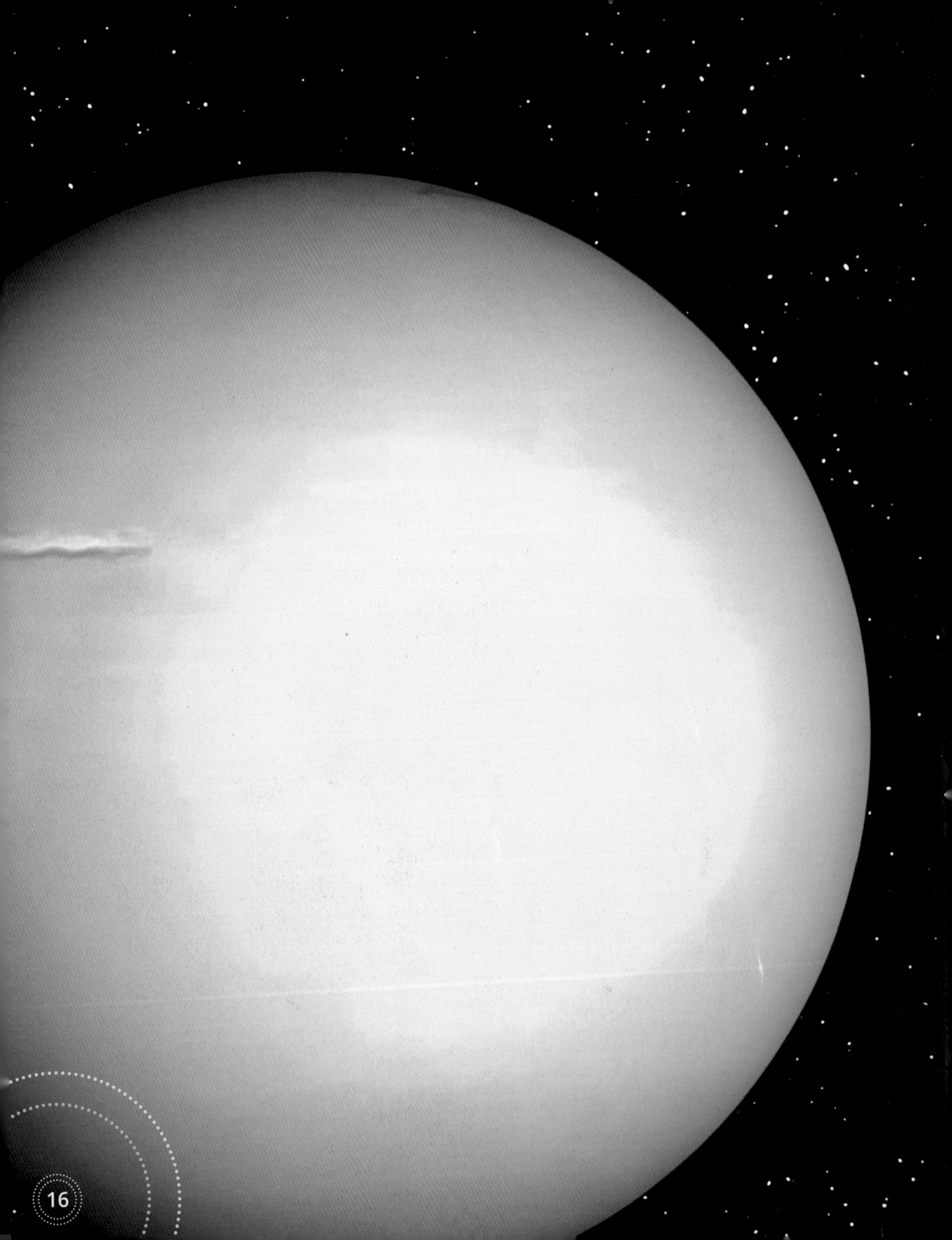

Uranus
and
Earth

Earth has very little in common with Uranus. In size, Uranus dwarfs Earth. In addition, Earth is a mostly solid ball surrounded by a blanket of gases. Uranus is a ball of gas with no solid surface. And no place on Earth experiences temperatures as cold as those found at the cloud tops of Uranus.

The distance between Earth and Uranus changes because the planets are always in motion. Earth is never closer to Uranus than 1.6 billion miles (2.6 billion kilometers). At their farthest, Earth and Uranus are separated by 1.98 billion miles (3.2 billion kilometers).

Next to Earth, Uranus looks like a giant. Earth's diameter, at 7,926 miles (12,756 kilometers), is about four times smaller than that of Uranus.

An **Icy** Planet

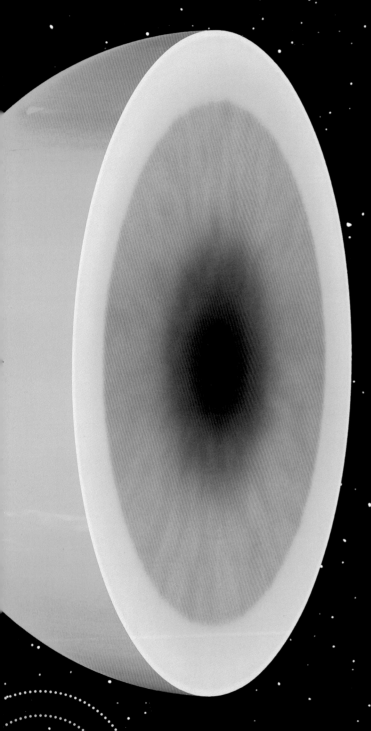

Astronomers have found that Uranus is a giant ball of gas and liquid. It does not have a solid outer surface, as Earth does. Like Saturn, Uranus has an outer layer made mostly of hydrogen and helium gas. The top of this layer consists of blue-green clouds formed of methane crystals.

But most of the mass of Uranus is made up of liquid. The liquid is mostly water and slushy ammonia and methane ice.

At the very center of Uranus may be a *molten* (melted) rocky core about the size of Earth. Scientists think the core of Uranus may be as hot as 12,600 °F (7000 °C).

Even with such a hot core, Uranus produces less internal heat than the other gas giants. In fact, Uranus releases as much heat into space as it receives from the sun.

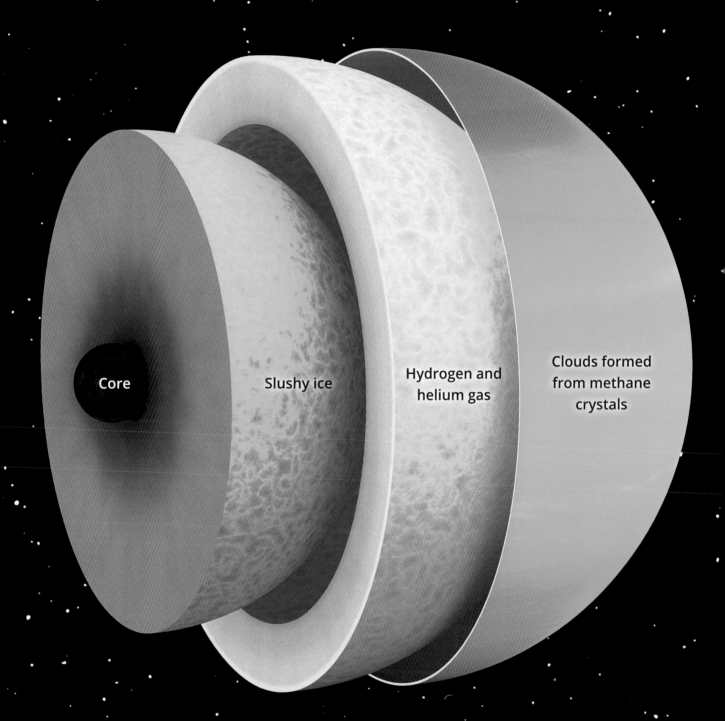

A World Tipped Over

Perhaps the biggest difference between Uranus and the other planets of the solar system is the tilt of Uranus's axis. Uranus is tilted so far on its side that its equator is nearly sideways. It is a world tipped over!

How did this happen? Some astronomers think that long ago another planet—perhaps larger than Earth—slammed into Uranus and knocked it onto its side. Because Uranus is a giant ball of gas and slushy ice, it would not have shattered into pieces. But it may have been knocked over!

Other astronomers think that the **gravitational** pull of a large **moon** or a passing planet that has since moved on caused the ice giant to tip over on its side.

This unique tilt of Uranus causes the most extreme seasons in the solar system. Each season—spring, summer, autumn, and winter—lasts almost 20 Earth years. Because Uranus's axis is tilted far on its side, the sun shines directly on one polar area in summer and winter. The other polar region of the planet experiences a long winter in darkness!

Pale Stripes and Clouds of Rotten Eggs

From Earth, Uranus always looks like a pale blue ball in space. But images taken with powerful new telescopes reveal faint bands in the atmosphere of Uranus. The bands are much like those seen on Jupiter and Saturn. The lighter bands form as gases within a region warm and rise. Gases in the atmosphere of Uranus cool and sink in other regions to make slightly darker bands.

The faint stripes rotate around the equator of Uranus. They do this even though the planet is tipped over on its axis compared with the other planets.

Only in 1986 did astronomers first observe that Uranus has faint clouds. The composition of the clouds on Uranus has long been a mystery to astronomers. In 2017, astronomers analyzed the light reflected from the clouds on Uranus to determine what they were made of. They found that the clouds on Uranus are composed of hydrogen sulfide. This poisonous gas smells just like rotten eggs!

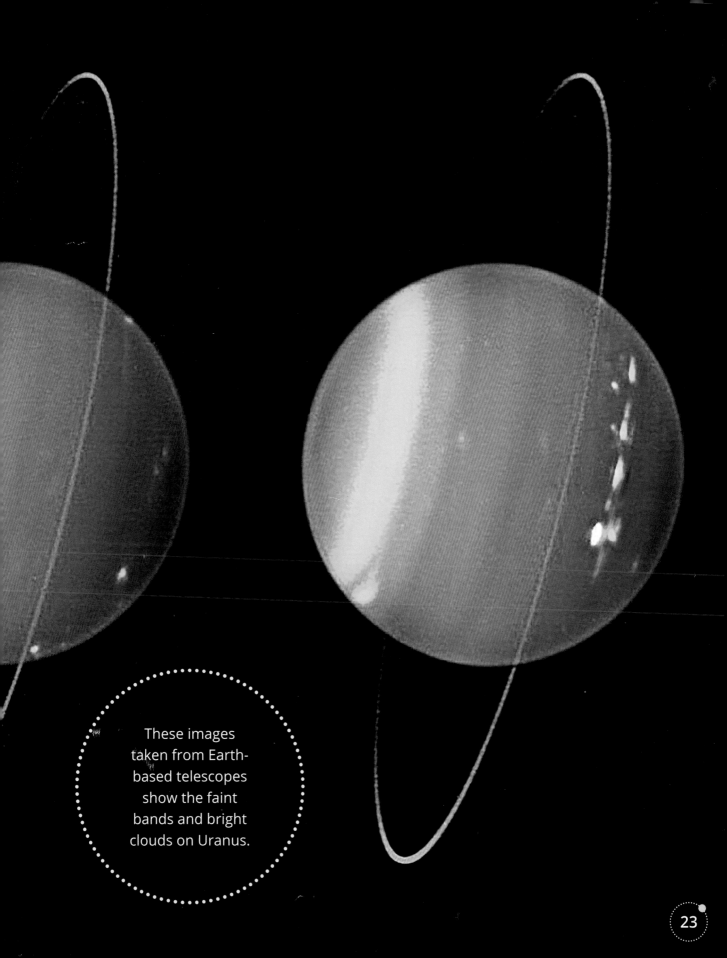

These images taken from Earth-based telescopes show the faint bands and bright clouds on Uranus.

Weather
on Uranus

The extreme tilt of Uranus, its distance from the sun, and the long length of its year make for some odd weather on the ice giant.

On most planets, the equator receives the most sunlight over the course of a year. This warms the air, which then rises and moves to the poles, where the air then cools and sinks. This movement of air across a planet drives the planet's weather.

But the equator of Uranus hardly ever faces the sun. This shows that the weather on Uranus is not driven by temperature changes caused by sunlight. Scientists think that the weather on Uranus is driven mainly by the heat given off from the planet itself. Winds distribute heat fairly evenly throughout the atmosphere of Uranus.

A storm circling the polar region of Uranus shows up as a bright white spot.

But Uranus is not a warm place! The planet has an average temperature of −323 °F (−197 °C). The upper atmosphere on Uranus is far colder. Scientists have measured a temperature as cold as −371 °F (−224 °C) at the cloud tops of Uranus.

Astronomers have seen storms that appear as darker spots on the pale blue surface of Uranus. Winds may howl around the southern half of Uranus at more than 560 miles (900 kilometers) per hour!

Uranus Has
Rings!

In 1977—nearly 200 years after Uranus was discovered—astronomers found that Uranus has a system of faint rings! Astronomers sighted the rings when Uranus passed in front of a distant star. The rings around Uranus are only visible when viewed through a powerful telescope.

Astronomers have since counted at least 13 rings circling Uranus. Unlike the bright rings of Saturn, which are easily seen when viewed with a simple telescope, the rings of Uranus are rather thin and dark. This makes them hard to see. The rings cannot be seen in most photographs of Uranus.

The rings of Uranus range in width from less than 3 miles (5 kilometers) to 60 miles (100 kilometers). They are no more than 33 feet (10 meters) thick.

Astronomers think the rings of Uranus are made of chunks of ice covered in a layer of **carbon.** Because the axis of Uranus is tilted sideways, the planet's equator encircles it from top to bottom. Uranus's rings also run from top to bottom. On other planets, the equator runs from side to side. Uranus looks different from Saturn, which wears its rings like a big, beautiful belt.

An artist's illustration shows a close-up view of the rings of Uranus.

The tiny moon
Puck seen in
front of Uranus

The **Moons** of Uranus

Uranus has at least 27 moons, but more will probably be discovered. Most of Uranus's moons are small, and their surfaces are marked with craters. Uranus has no giant moons like Jupiter's moon Ganymede or Saturn's moon Titan.

Uranus's moon Miranda is one of the strangest objects in the solar system. It has three large, oddly shaped regions called *ovoids.* The outer areas of each ovoid look like a race track. They have parallel ridges and canyons wrapped around the center. Ridges and canyons crisscross one another in the center.

Some of the canyons are 12 times as deep as Earth's Grand Canyon. Another odd formation on Miranda is called a *chevron (SHEV rohn).* It looks like a huge letter *V.*

Uranus's moon Miranda has surface features not seen anywhere else in the solar system.

Uranus's moons Cordelia and Ophelia are known as *shepherd moons*. As they orbit the planet, their gravitational pull keeps the faint rings of Uranus in order. They keep pieces of the ring from "wandering away" into space.

The names of Uranus's moons do not follow the same naming convention as other planets in the solar system. The moons are not named for gods from the myths of ancient Greece or Rome.

Instead, most of the moons of Uranus are named for characters from the works of the English playwright William Shakespeare. Among these characters are Oberon and Titania from *A Midsummer Night's Dream;* Desdemona from *Othello;* Ophelia from *Hamlet;* and Ariel and Caliban from *The Tempest.*

An artist's view of the shepherd moons around Uranus

Exploring
Uranus

Distant Uranus appears as a nearly featureless pale blue ball in space when viewed with a telescope. Uranus has been visited by only one space probe from Earth. In 1986, Voyager 2 passed within 50,600 miles (80,000 kilometers) of Uranus. The probe had been launched from Earth by the United States National Aeronautics and Space Administration (NASA) in 1977. Before it arrived at Uranus, the probe had previously studied Jupiter and Saturn.

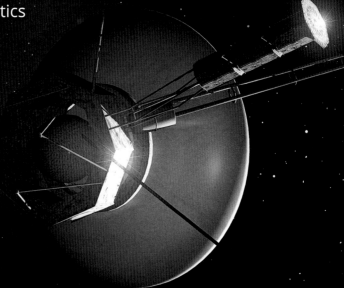

Voyager 2 spent only six hours studying Uranus. But the probe sent streams of *data* (information) back to Earth. Voyager 2 detected a magnetic field around Uranus, which scientists had not known about before. Voyager 2 also collected a vast amount of new information about the faint rings of Uranus.

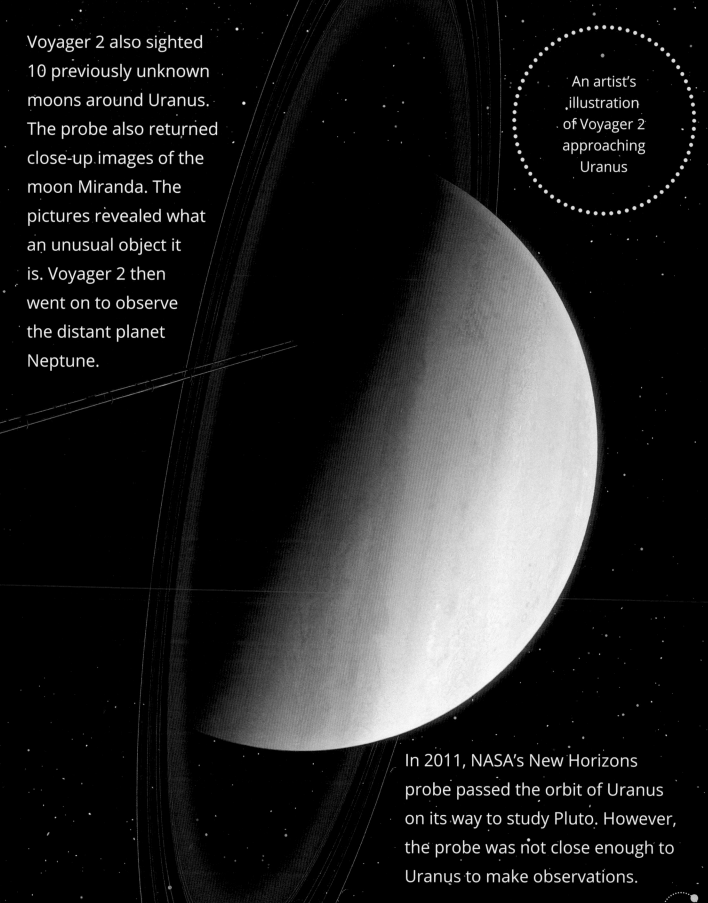

Voyager 2 also sighted 10 previously unknown moons around Uranus. The probe also returned close-up images of the moon Miranda. The pictures revealed what an unusual object it is. Voyager 2 then went on to observe the distant planet Neptune.

An artist's illustration of Voyager 2 approaching Uranus

In 2011, NASA's New Horizons probe passed the orbit of Uranus on its way to study Pluto. However, the probe was not close enough to Uranus to make observations.

Deep Blue
Neptune

Deep blue Neptune is a remote and mysterious world. It is the most distant planet from the sun in our solar system. It receives little light or warmth from the sun. The sun is so far away that the sky on Neptune at midday is about as dim as a sunset here on Earth.

Neptune is the only planet in our solar system that cannot be seen from Earth without a telescope. When viewed through a simple telescope, Neptune appears as a bright point in the sky, like a star.

In photographs taken from space
by probes and more powerful
telescopes, Neptune looks like a
giant blue ball with tiny wisps of
white clouds.

Neptune's orbit lies beyond
the orbit of Uranus, its inner
neighbor. Like Uranus, Neptune
is an ice giant. The part of
Neptune that we can see is made
up of layers of clouds. Deeper in,
compressed (squeezed together)
gases form a dense, slushy liquid
that makes up most of the planet.

The **Outermost** Planet

Pluto

Neptune is **so far away** from the sun that it takes light four hours and six minutes to reach it.

Neptune's
average distance
from the sun
is about 2.8 billion miles (4.5 billion kilometers). At its closest distance, Neptune lies about 2.7 billion miles (4.3 billion kilometers) from Earth.

Neptune may be the outermost planet in the solar system, but some smaller objects orbit
even farther away,
such as some comets, **dwarf planets,** and other icy, rocky bodies.

The dwarf planet Pluto has a highly oval-shaped orbit which brings it
inside
Neptune's orbit
every 248 Earth years. Neptune is then farther from the sun than Pluto for about 20 Earth years. But the two orbit in such a way that keeps them from ever crashing into each other.

Neptune

Orbit of Neptune

Orbit of Pluto

Discovery
of Neptune

Neptune was the first planet discovered by means of mathematics rather than by observations of the sky.

Since Neptune cannot be seen in the sky without a telescope, this planet was unknown to people in ancient times. The Italian astronomer Galileo *(GAL uh LAY oh)* probably spotted Neptune in 1612, using a simple telescope. However, he thought the tiny point of light was a distant star.

In the 1800's, the astronomers John C. Adams of England and Urbain J. J. Le Verrier *(luh VEHR ee ay)* of France noticed unusual changes in the orbit of the planet Uranus. They calculated that the changes were caused by the gravitational pull of another planet orbiting beyond Uranus. Le Verrier used the calculations to predict where this unknown planet could be found in the night sky.

The German astronomers Johann G. Galle *(GAHL uh)* and Heinrich L. d'Arrest *(duh REST)* followed those predictions. On Sept. 23, 1846, they found Neptune after only 30 minutes of searching the sky using a telescope. The planet was seen in the sky at almost exactly the position predicted by Le Verrier.

Astronomers named the new planet for Neptune, the Roman god of the sea. The name fits well, for the planet is deep blue in color, just like the sea.

Icy Twins

Neptune is one of two ice giants in the outer solar system. Uranus is the other. Neptune is the fourth largest planet in the solar system. Only Jupiter, Saturn, and Uranus are larger.

Uranus is only slightly larger than Neptune. If the two planets were side by side, you would have to look closely to see any difference in size. The two planets have similar colors, interior structures,

Neptune

masses, and densities. Astronomers sometimes refer to these two cold, distant worlds as twin planets.

Like Uranus, Neptune is made of a thick soup of water, ammonia, and methane over an Earth-sized solid center. Its atmosphere is made of hydrogen, helium, and methane. The methane gives Neptune the same blue color as Uranus. But Neptune is a darker shade of blue.

Uranus

Neptune
Composition

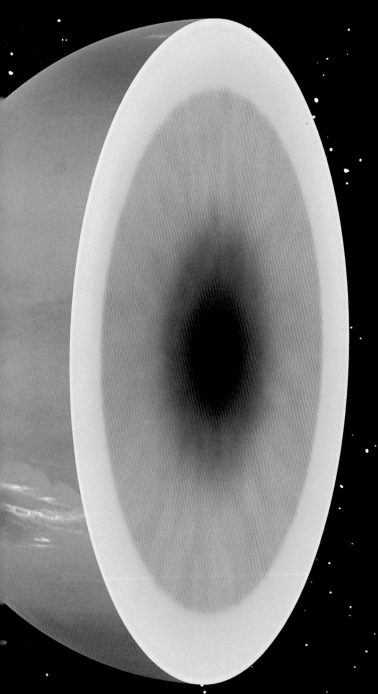

Neptune is made up mostly of hydrogen, helium, water, methane, and ammonia. Unlike Earth, Neptune has no solid ground. The part of Neptune that we can see is made up of layers of clouds. Deeper within, there is a layer of compressed gases.

Farther inside the planet, in the layer known as the mantle, the gases blend into a layer of liquid. Some scientists think that this liquid layer might be superheated water. The water is so hot that it would boil away if it could. But the pressure of the surrounding gases keeps it liquid. Inside the mantle is most likely a solid core made of ice and rock.

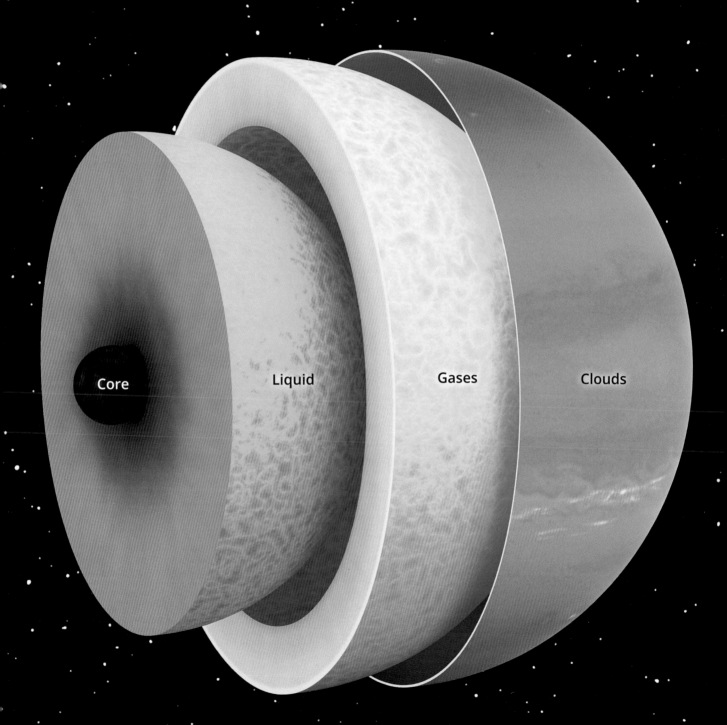

Neptune and the **Sun**

Like the other planets in the solar system, Neptune travels in an

elliptical orbit

around the sun. However, Neptune's orbit is closer to a perfect circle than the oval-shaped orbits of most other planets in our solar system.

Because Neptune is so far from the sun, it takes Neptune 60,190 Earth days to complete one orbit. That is about

165 Earth years!

With a year that long, New Year's celebrations on Neptune would be few and far between.

FUN FACT

In 2011, Neptune completed its

first orbit

around the sun since it was discovered in 1846.

Although a year on Neptune is much longer than a year on Earth,

Neptune's day

is much shorter. Neptune's day equals 16 hours and 7 minutes on Earth. That is how long it takes Neptune to rotate on its axis once. Neptune's day is shorter because the planet rotates faster than Earth does.

Neptune is tilted on its axis much like Mars and Earth. This means that Neptune

experiences seasons

just like we do on Earth.

Weather
on Neptune

The weather on Neptune is cloudy, windy, and cold. The average temperature of Neptune's outer cloud layer is –355 °F (–215 °C). High in Neptune's atmosphere, thick layers of clouds are in rapid motion. Winds blow these clouds at speeds up to about 900 miles (1,450 kilometers) per hour.

Unlike the winds on the other giant planets, Neptune's winds tend to blow in the opposite direction of the planet's rotation. The highest clouds in Neptune's atmosphere consist mainly of frozen methane. Astronomers have observed dark areas of violently swirling gas occasionally appearing on Neptune. These are most likely huge storms that resemble a hurricane.

Scientists have found evidence that Neptune has four seasons, just as Earth does. On Neptune, a season is not three months long, as it is on Earth. Instead, a season lasts for more than 40 Earth years.

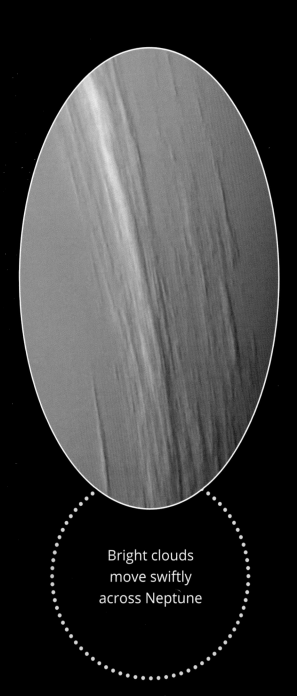

Bright clouds move swiftly across Neptune

Neptune's clouds move in the opposite direction of the planet's rotation.

FUN FACT

In 2011, Neptune astronomers named one of the clouds that floats above Neptune

Scooter.

The little cloud "scoots" quickly around the planet about once every 16 hours.

Neptune and Earth

AT A GLANCE

Next to Earth, Neptune would appear huge. If Neptune were hollow, it would take about

58 planets
the size of Earth

to fill it up.

The diameter of Neptune at its equator is 30,775 miles (49,528 kilometers).

That is nearly
four times
the diameter of Earth.

Neptune has about

17 times

as much mass as Earth. However, its average density is only about 1.5 times as great as Earth's because Neptune consists mainly of gas.

Neptune's
surface gravity

is slightly greater than Earth's. If you weighed 100 pounds (45 kilograms) on Earth, you would weigh about 112 pounds (51 kilograms) on Neptune.

112

Earth receives a lot of heat from the sun. The heat keeps Earth and the living things on it warm. But Neptune is on the outer edge of the solar system. It receives only a tiny fraction of the sunlight that bathes Earth. Viewed from Earth,

the sun is 900 times as bright

as it appears from Neptune.

Neptune's
Rings

Astronomers did not know Neptune had rings until 1984. In that year, they watched the planet through a telescope as it passed in front of a distant star. The starlight "winked" (dimmed and then brightened) when it crossed a ring. The rings are very thin and faint, so they do not show up in most photographs of Neptune.

Astronomers have counted at least five faint rings circling the equator of Neptune. The rings are probably made of dust.

Neptune's rings also have clumps of dust in sections, called arcs, that shine more brightly than other parts of the ring. Scientists believe that dust may be gathered more thickly in these sections.

One of Neptune's moons, Galatea *(gal uh TEE uh),* orbits the planet just inside the outermost ring. Its gravitational pull probably causes dust to clump into the three bright arcs seen in that ring.

Moons
of Neptune

Neptune has at least 13 moons. The three largest moons are Triton *(TRY tuhn),* Proteus *(PROH tee uhs),* and Nereid *(NIHR ee ihd).* Triton is one of the larger moons in the solar system, but Neptune's other moons are quite small.

Proteus, Neptune's second largest moon, is dark and very close to the planet. Astronomers using telescopes on Earth did not see this small moon. The space probe Voyager 2 sent back photographs of Proteus when it visited Neptune in 1989.

Nereid, Neptune's third largest moon, has an orbit that is the most elliptical of any moon in the solar system. Proteus, Nereid, and Neptune's other small moons are all less than 300 miles (480 kilometers) in diameter.

Neptune's moon Hippocamp in front of the ice giant planet Neptune

FUN FACT

In 2013, a scientist studying images of Neptune taken by the Hubble Space Telescope discovered a previously unknown

14th moon

of Neptune. This moon has the designation S/2004 N 1 until the discovery is confirmed. Then, the moon will be given a name.

Exploring
Neptune

Only one space mission has ever visited Neptune. In 1977, NASA launched a probe called Voyager 2. On Aug. 25, 1989, the probe passed within about 3,000 miles (4,850 kilometers) of the cloud-covered surface of Neptune. That was 3 ½ years after Voyager 2 flew past Uranus; 8 years after the probe visited Saturn; and 10 years after Voyager 2's journey past Jupiter.

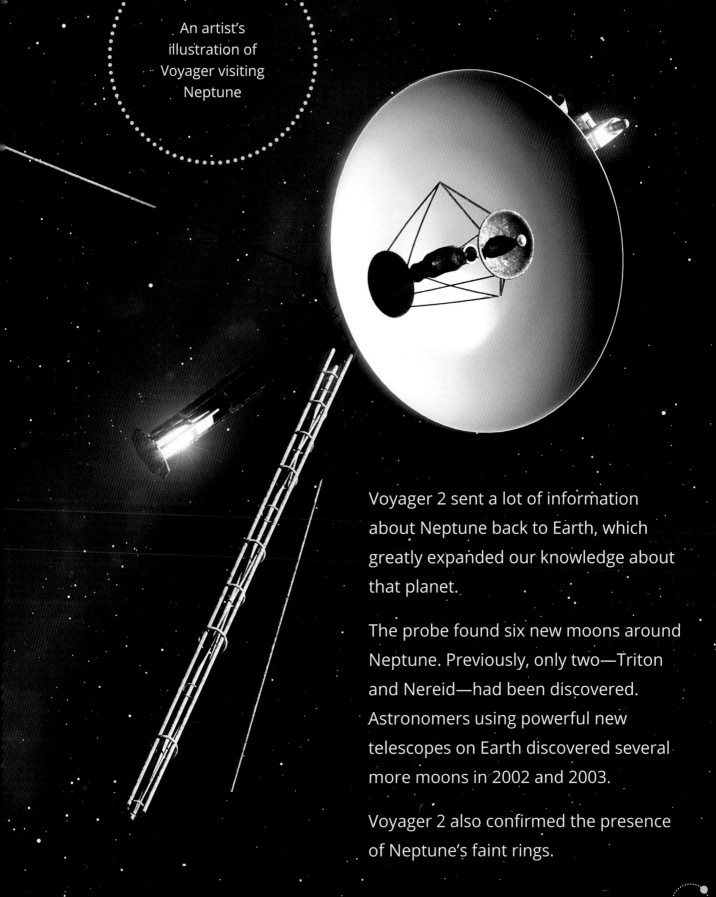

An artist's illustration of Voyager visiting Neptune

Voyager 2 sent a lot of information about Neptune back to Earth, which greatly expanded our knowledge about that planet.

The probe found six new moons around Neptune. Previously, only two—Triton and Nereid—had been discovered. Astronomers using powerful new telescopes on Earth discovered several more moons in 2002 and 2003.

Voyager 2 also confirmed the presence of Neptune's faint rings.

Mysterious
Triton

Triton is Neptune's largest moon. It has a diameter of about 1,680 miles (2,700 kilometers). It is one of the larger moons in the solar system. Only Jupiter's four largest moons, Earth's moon, and Saturn's moon Titan are larger.

The surface of Triton is rough and icy. Like Saturn's moon Titan—and unlike most other moons in our solar system—Triton has an atmosphere. Its atmosphere is made mainly of nitrogen gas.

Triton is one of the coldest places in the entire solar system! The surface temperature is about –390 °F (–235 °C).

Triton also has *geysers*—plumes of liquid nitrogen, methane, and dust that sometimes spurt from beneath its surface. They are like ice volcanoes! The plumes shoot as high as 5 miles (8 kilometers) above the surface. The liquid freezes instantly and falls onto the surface of Triton like snow.

Triton orbits Neptune in the opposite direction of Neptune's rotation. That is why many scientists think Triton was a rocky body that was captured by Neptune's gravity long after the planet formed. Triton's orbit is slowly bringing it closer to Neptune. Billions of years from now, Triton may break up and form a new ring around Neptune.

Neptune's moon Triton in front of the ice giant planet

Triton was discovered

only 17 days after astronomers first sighted Neptune itself, in 1846.

Life
on an Ice Giant?

Scientists believe there is very little chance of finding any kind of life on the ice giants Uranus or Neptune or their moons.

The atmospheres of these twin planets are made up of gases that would be poisonous if breathed by the living things we know about. In addition, the pressure of those gases is so immensely strong, it would crush any living things.

Finally, the temperatures on these giant planets are incredibly cold—much colder than any place where life exists on Earth.

Neptune's only moon with an atmosphere is Triton. But it is very hard to imagine life as we know it on Triton with the extremely cold temperatures it has. The coldest places on Earth—areas of Antarctica—would seem warm and inviting compared to frigid Triton.

There may be life somewhere in the universe other than on Earth. But it is not likely to be found on or near Uranus or Neptune.

An artist's illustration shows a sunrise on frigid Triton with Neptune nearby.

Glossary

ammonia A colorless gas, consisting of one part nitrogen and three parts hydrogen. Ammonia has a very strong and suffocating smell.

astronomer A scientist who studies stars, planets, and other objects or forces in space.

atmosphere *(AT muh sfihr)* The mass of gases that surrounds a planet or other body.

axis In planets, the imaginary line about which the planet seems to turn, or rotate.

carbon A common chemical element that is black in color. Carbon occurs in combination with other elements in all plants and animals.

comet A small body made of dirt and ice that orbits the sun.

core The center part of the inside of a planet, moon, or star.

day The time it takes a planet to *rotate* (spin) once around its axis and come back to the same position in relation to the sun.

density The amount of matter in a given space.

diameter The length of a straight line through the middle of a circle or anything shaped like a ball.

dwarf planet A rounded body in space orbiting a star, which does not have enough gravitational pull to clear other objects from its orbit.

equator An imaginary circle around the middle of a planet.

gravity The force of attraction that acts between all objects because of their mass.

helium A lightweight chemical element. Helium is the second most abundant element in the universe.

hydrogen The most abundant chemical element in the universe.

mantle The area of a planet or moon between the crust and the core.

mass The amount of matter that an object has.

methane A compound formed of the chemical elements carbon and hydrogen.

moon A smaller body that orbits a planet or asteroid.

mythology Certain types of legends or stories.

orbit The path that a smaller body takes around a larger body; for instance, the path that a planet takes around the sun.

planet A large, round body in space that orbits a star. A planet must have sufficient gravitational pull to clear other objects from the area of its orbit.

pole A point on any revolving sphere.

probe An unpiloted device sent to explore space. Most probes send *data* (information) from space back to Earth.

solar system A group of bodies in space made up of a star and the planets and other objects orbiting around that star.

star A huge, shining ball in space that produces a great amount of visible light and other forms of energy.

telescope An instrument for making distant objects appear nearer and larger. Simple telescopes usually consist of an arrangement of lenses, and sometimes mirrors, in one or more tubes.

volume The space occupied by an object.

year The time it takes a planet to complete one orbit around the sun.

Index

World Book, Inc.
180 North LaSalle Street
Suite 900
Chicago, Illinois 60601
USA

For information about other "Solar System" titles, as well as other World Book print and digital publications, please go to www.worldbook.com or call 1-800-WORLDBK (967-5325).

For information about sales to schools and libraries, call 1-800-975-3250 (United States) or 1-800-837-5365 (Canada).

Library of Congress Cataloging-in-Publication Data for this volume has been applied for.

Our Solar System
ISBN: 978-0-7166-8058-1 (set, hc.)

Uranus and Neptune: The Ice Giants
ISBN: 978-0-7166-8065-9 (hc.)

Also available as:
ISBN: 978-0-7166-8075-8 (e-book)

Printed in India
by Thomson Press (India) Limited
Uttar Pradesh, India
2nd printing September 2021

Staff

Editorial

Writer
Nicholas Kilzer

Senior Editor
Shawn Brennan

Editors
Will Adams
Mellonee Carrigan

Proofreader
Nathalie Strassheim

Manager, Indexing Services
David Pofelski

Graphics and Design

Senior Visual Communications Designer
Melanie Bender

Media Editor
Rosalia Bledsoe

Acknowledgments

Cover: © Jurik Peter, Shutterstock; NASA/JPL-Caltech; NASA/JPL
1   NASA/JPL-Caltech; NASA/JPL
2-3   © Shutterstock
4-5   NASA/JPL
6-7   NASA/JPL-Caltech; © Nostalgia for Infinity/Shutterstock
8-9   © North Wind Picture Archives/Alamy Images; © Cory Thoman, Shutterstock
10-17 © Shutterstock
18-19 © Mark Garlick, Science Photo Library/Getty Images
20-21 © SCIEPRO/Getty Images
22-23 NASA/Lawrence Sromovsky, University of Wisconsin-Madison/W. W. Keck Observatory
24-25 © Shutterstock; NASA/Space Telescope Science Institute Office of Public Outreach
26-27 © Mark Garlick, Science Source
28-29 © Stocktrek Images/Getty Images; NASA/JPL-Caltech
30-31 © John R. Foster, Science Source
32-33 © Mark Garlick, Science Source
34-35 NASA/JPL
36-41 © Shutterstock
42-43 © Mark Garlick, Science Photo Library/Getty Images
44-45 © Andamati/Shutterstock
46-47 NASA/JPL
48-49 © Shutterstock
50-51 © Mark Garlick, Science Photo Library/Getty Images
52-53 ESA/Hubble/NASA/L. Calçada
54-55 © Mark Garlick, Science Source
56-57 NASA/JPL/USGS
58-59 © Detlev van Ravenswaay, Science Photo Library/Getty Images